ADVENTURES IN NATURE

EXPLORING THE SEASIDE

BY JEN GREEN AND LIA VISIRIN

WINDMILL BOOKS

Published in 2026 by Windmill Books,
an Imprint of Rosen Publishing
2544 Clinton St.
Buffalo, NY 14224

First published in Great Britain in 2025 by Hodder & Stoughton

Credits
Series Editor: Grace Kelly
Series Designer: Peter Scoulding

Cataloging-in-Publication Data
Names: Green, Jen, author. | Visirin, Lia, illustrator.
Title: Exploring the seaside / Jen Green, illustrated by Lia Visirin.
Description: Buffalo, NY : Windmill Books, 2026. | Series: Adventures in nature | Includes glossary and index.
Identifiers: ISBN 9781538398777 (pbk.) | ISBN 9781538398784 (library bound) | ISBN 9781538398791 (ebook)
Subjects: LCSH: Beaches--Juvenile literature. | Seashore animals--Juvenile literature. | Nature study--Juvenile literature.
Classification: LCC GB453.G743 2026 | DDC 796.5'3--dc23

Printed in the United States of America

CPSIA Compliance Information: Batch #CSWM26
For Further Information contact Rosen Publishing at 1-800-237-9932

CONTENTS

AT THE SEASIDE

The seaside is the place where the land meets the ocean. Many different kinds of scenery can be found here, including cliffs, rocky shores, sand or pebble beaches, dunes, and mudflats. Each of these places provides a habitat for different plants and animals.

Seaside animals, such as crabs, are shy and good at hiding, so you have to look for them carefully. Sudden movements can scare them away.

Looking for nature at the seaside, you will need waterproof clothing and boots, a hat, and sunscreen.

Make notes and drawings using a notebook, pen, and colored pencils. A magnifying glass, phone camera, fishing net, and a collecting jar can also be useful.

This symbol warns when extra care is needed. Always take care of nature. Never pick plants and don't handle wild creatures.

BETWEEN THE TIDES

Twice a day, the sea moves up the shore and then falls back again. These changes are called tides. Seaside plants and animals have to cope with ever-changing conditions, as they are covered with salty seawater and then left high and dry!

The beach is the area found between the high and low tide mark.

At high tide, waves lap at the top of the beach. The lowest part of the beach is covered with water, except at very low tide.

To stay safe at the seaside, always check what the tide is doing. Remember, the tide can rise quickly. The times of the tides are different every day.

A line of seaweed and shells is left at the high tide – the highest level reached by the waves.

WHAT DO YOU SEE?

Walk from the top of the beach down toward the water. The upper, middle, and lower shore will each have different plants and animals. Use your notebook to record the ones you can see in each zone.

IF YOU HAVE VISITED THE SEASIDE BEFORE, WAS IT HIGH OR LOW TIDE? HOW COULD YOU TELL?

ON THE CLIFFS

Cliffs form where a line of hills meets the sea. Clifftops are often grassy, and dotted with flowers in spring and summer. Rabbits sometimes live in clifftop burrows. Seabirds perch on ledges halfway down!

Different types of bird nest on cliffs.

PUFFINS LIVE IN BURROWS NEAR THE TOP OF CLIFFS.

GUILLEMOTS LAY THEIR EGGS ON NARROW LEDGES.

KITTIWAKES BUILD SEAWEED NESTS ON STEEP CLIFFS.

GANNETS RAISE ONE CHICK IN A NEST MADE OF SEAWEED.

WHAT DO YOU SEE?

Binoculars will help you study cliff birds. A bird book or website can help you to identify them. What were the birds doing?

Seabirds such as these black-headed gulls nest on cliffs where their eggs and young are safe from most predators.

Clifftop plants have to cope with strong winds and salty air. This plant is called thrift.

Gorse often grows on a cliff edge.

Insects visit clifftop plants for food.

Cliff edges can crumble away suddenly. Never stand close to the edge, or on the beach directly below a cliff.

PEBBLE BEACH

Pebbles on the beach are made of rocks worn smooth by the waves. The stones mostly come from local cliffs, or have been swept along the coast by the tide. Pebble beaches are home to tough plants that can stand salty conditions, and birds such as plovers and oystercatchers.

Plants that grow among the pebbles survive with very little soil. This is sea bindweed.

As waves grind small chunks of rock, they become smooth, rounded pebbles.

Watch out for broken glass or rusty cans among the pebbles.

CAN YOU FIND ANY PEBBLES MADE FROM SMOOTH GLASS?

Plover birds are well camouflaged against gray, black, and brown pebbles. They lure underground prey by tapping their feet on the rocks, then snap them up!

WHAT DO YOU SEE?

Make a collection of pebbles. Most are probably made of one type of rock. Can you see the same type of rock on nearby cliffs?

Beach pebbles come in a variety of different colors, depending on the rock they are made of. Gray pebbles are often made of shale or slate, yellowish ones from limestone, white or pinkish pebbles from quartz.

BIRDS ON THE SHORE

Birds that live at the seaside find their food in different places. Terns and gannets dive underwater to catch fish. Oystercatchers wade at the water's edge. Turnstones hunt at the high-tide mark. Seashore birds have specially shaped beaks, legs, and feet, which help them move around and catch their food.

These birds can often be found feeding on the seashore.

A GULL'S HOOKED BEAK GRIPS SLIPPERY FISH.

A TURNSTONE FLIPS OVER PEBBLES IN SEARCH OF FOOD.

AN OYSTERCATCHER PROBES FOR WORMS WITH ITS LONG BILL.

A gull's webbed feet push against the water, moving the gull forward. Birds with webbed feet are strong swimmers.

DO THE BIRDS YOU SEE ON THE SEASHORE HAVE WEBBED FEET?

WHAT DO YOU SEE?

Prints in the sand can be used to identify birds. Compare the prints you find with the ones shown here.

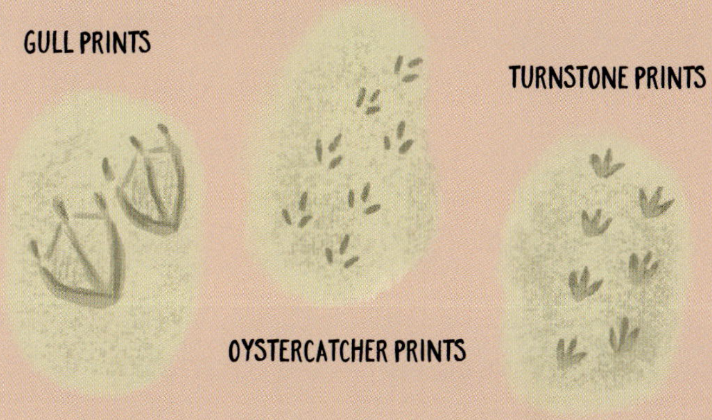

Young seagulls have different colored feathers than adult seagulls.

PLANTS OF THE SEA

Seaweeds are the main group of plants found at the seashore. There are also tiny floating plants called plankton. These sea plants don't have stems, leaves, and roots like the plants you see on land. But like all plants, they need sunlight to live and grow.

Seaweed can make rocks slippery so take care when walking on rocks and around rock pools.

WHAT DO YOU SEE?

Seaweeds come in three main colors: red, green, and brown. What color seaweed have you seen at the seaside?

This seaweed is brown kelp. Seaweeds such as kelp anchor themselves to rocks using a root-like part called a holdfast.

Bladderwrack is often found halfway down the beach. Air-filled pouches called bladders help the fronds to float.

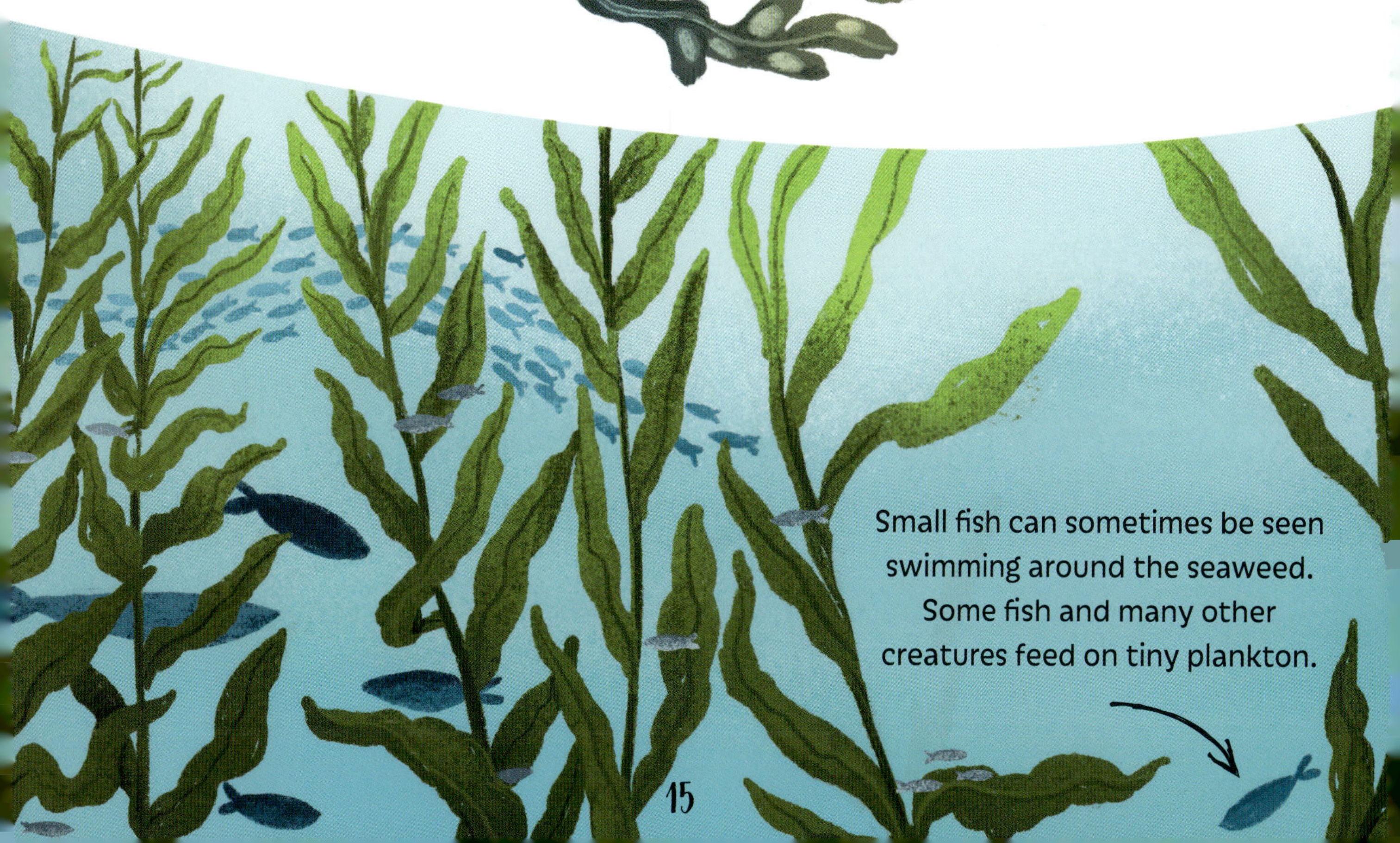

Small fish can sometimes be seen swimming around the seaweed. Some fish and many other creatures feed on tiny plankton.

IN THE SAND

Sand is made from tiny bits of rock and shell that have been smashed to pieces by the waves. A sandy beach can look bare, but worms, shellfish, and many other creatures are hidden in the sand.

These worms and shellfish hide in the sand.

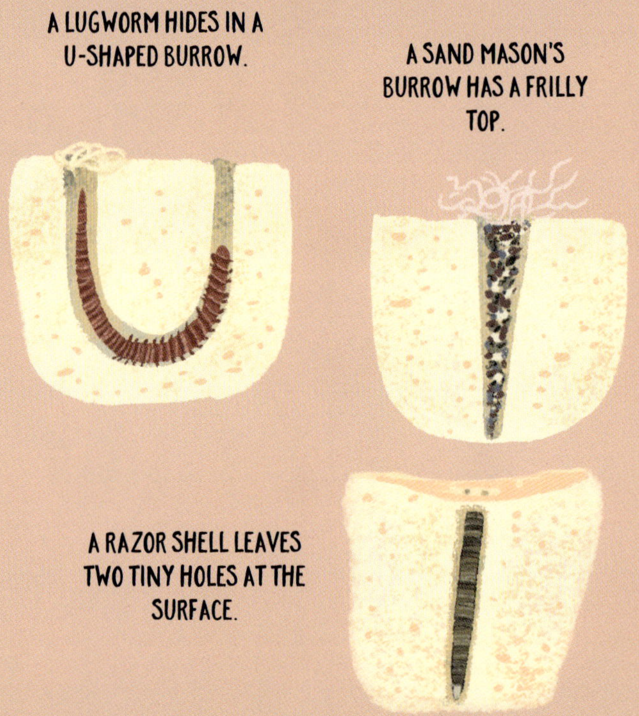

Shells can be found on sandy beaches.

WHAT DO YOU SEE?

Locate burrowing animals from the signs they leave at the surface. See if you can dig down quickly to identify the burrower, but don't disturb its work!

Lugworms swallow sand and filter out small bits of food. The waste sand is squeezed out to form a squiggly heap at the surface.

Crabs also burrow in the sand. Crabs are scavengers – they eat whatever they can find, from worms to other crabs!

AMONG THE DUNES

The wind blows loose sand to the back of the beach. There, it piles up to make heaps called sand dunes. Grass and other plants take root among the dunes. Some seabirds and many kinds of minibeast live here.

WHAT DO YOU SEE?

Make drawings of the dune plants you see in your notebook. Look carefully at the shape of leaves, stems, and flowers. Add color using pencils or pens.

Beachgrass has long roots to gather moisture. The roots also help to anchor the grass in the sand and hold the sand together.

Dune plants such as this thistle have tough, leathery leaves that keep in moisture. This prevents the plant from drying out in the salty air.

Sand dunes are rich in minibeasts. Wasps and bees burrow into the sand to lay their eggs, while butterflies visit to feed from dune plants, such as gorse.

HOW MANY DIFFERENT MINIBEASTS CAN YOU SEE IN THE DUNES?

IN THE SHALLOWS

All sorts of amazing shellfish live in the shallow waters just offshore. You will only see them at very low tide, or if they get washed up on the beach by accident. These animals spend most or all of their time underwater.

Oystercatchers hunt for shellfish, including oysters, on the rocks at low tide.

WHAT DO YOU SEE?

Limpets look fixed in one place, but at high tide they move. Make a note of one's position and see if it moves as the sea rises or falls.

Similarly, barnacles close up out of water. Put a small rock or pebble with a barnacle on it into a bucket of seawater and watch what happens!

Each limpet has a home base – a little groove in the rock. At high tide it moves around to eat seaweed.

Mussels can be seen stuck to the rocks at low tide, too.

IN A SHELL

Many seaside animals live inside a shell that protects their soft bodies. They are known as shellfish, and there are two main groups. Sea snails such as whelks, periwinkles, and scallops are mollusks.

Crabs, shrimps, and lobsters belong to a different group, called crustaceans. These many-legged creatures have a hard skin, like body armor.

These mollusk shells often wash up on the seashore.

PERIWINKLE

SCALLOP

LIMPET

RAZOR CLAM

Lobsters are crustaceans, with big, front claws and a hard body case.

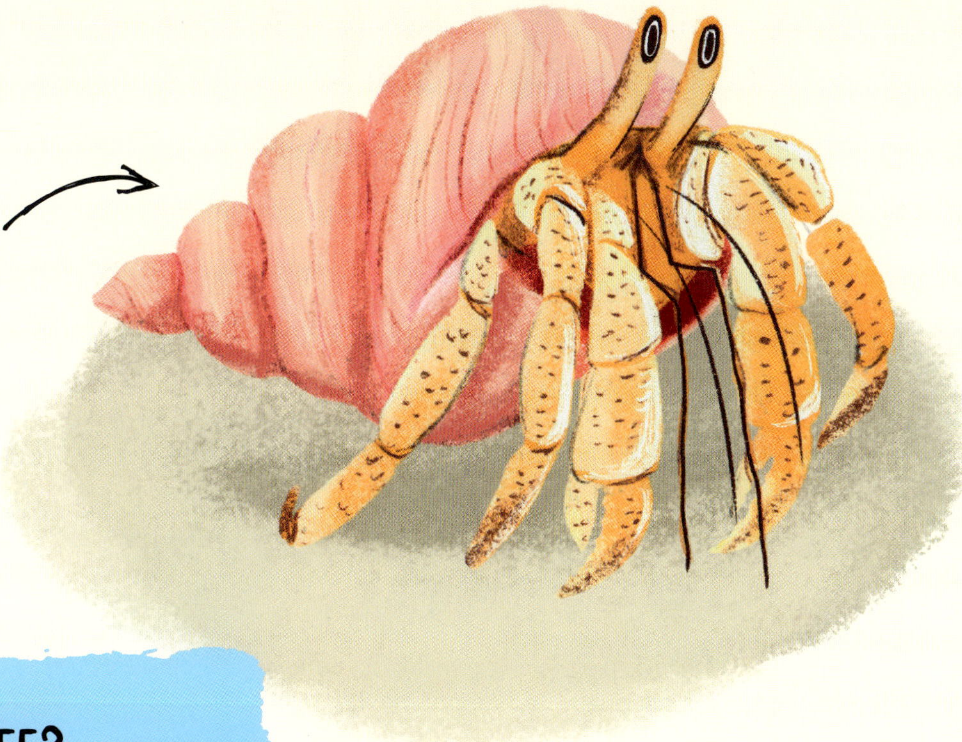

Unlike other crustaceans, the hermit crab has a soft body, so it hides inside another shell.

WHAT DO YOU SEE?

Make a collection of shells. Make sure there are no animals still living inside them! Can you group them according to their shape? Leave your collection behind when you go home, so new animals can shelter in them.

WHAT SHAPE ARE MOST OF THE SHELLS YOU HAVE FOUND?

A cockle has a double shell, joined together by a strong hinge.

IN A ROCK POOL

Rock pools form on rocky beaches when the tide goes out, leaving pools of salt water. Lots of different living things are found in rock pools, including seaweeds, anemones, prawns, mollusks, starfish, crabs, and small fish.

TRY THIS!

Study rock pool life by gently sweeping a net across a pool and along its bottom. Put the creatures you catch in a collecting jar filled with seawater while you study them. Put them back gently when you have finished.

Rock pools contain dozens of different living things, both big and small.

Take care on slippery rocks and be aware of rising tides.

Anemones capture their prey with their stinging tentacles.

These creatures are common in rock pools:

AN ANEMONE OFTEN LOOKS LIKE A BLOB OF JELLY AT LOW TIDE.

A COMMON PRAWN HAS BROWN STRIPES AND TWO LONG ANTENNAE.

A STARFISH HAS FIVE ARMS.

This small rock pool fish has a speckled body. This makes it hard to see among the rocks.

HOW MANY DIFFERENT ROCK POOL CREATURES CAN YOU FIND?

SEASIDE FOOD CHAINS

Living things on the seashore depend on one another for food. Diagrams called food chains show who eats what. Plants form the base of seaside food chains. They provide food for animals called herbivores. These may be eaten by meat-eating hunters, known as carnivores.

This gull is eating a crab. Crabs often feed on sandhoppers – shrimp-like creatures that eat rotting seaweed at the high tide mark.

This food chain shows the links between the gull, crab, sandhopper, and seaweed. The gull is the carnivore at the top of the chain.

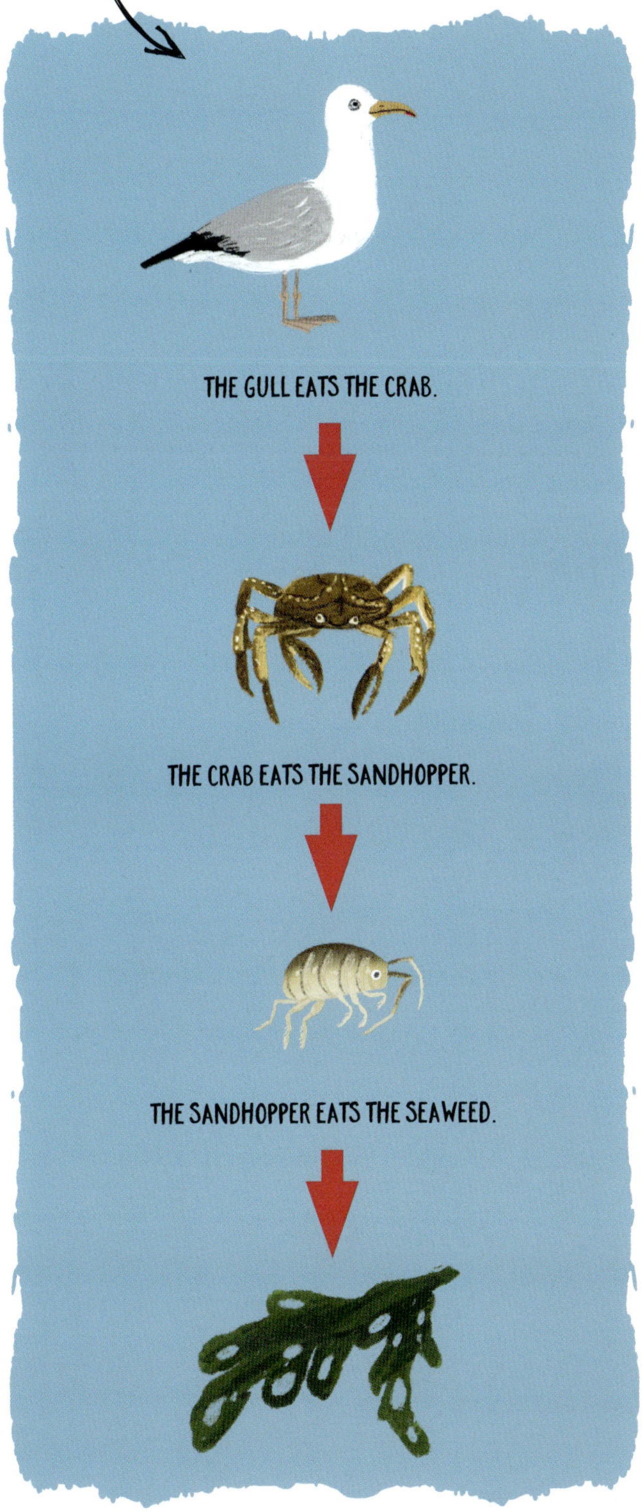

WHAT DO YOU SEE?

Look around and see if you can spot animals eating plants or other creatures. Try to draw a food chain showing the animals.

Seaweed provides food for many sea creatures. This bright green seaweed is called sea lettuce.

This long-tailed bird, a pied wagtail, is searching for food in the seaweed.

NATURE DIARY

Build up a detailed picture of life on the seashore in your notebook. Add drawings or photos. All sorts of amazing things wash up on beaches and each fresh tide brings new treasures!

KEEP NOTES

Always take your notebook with you. Record the date, time, weather, state of the tide, and place. Describe and draw what you see.

Can you identify these rock pool creatures? If you see a plant or animal you don't recognize, make notes and a sketch or take a photo. Look it up later in a book or website about seashore life.

TOP TIPS

- Use the cover of rocks or sand dunes to approach birds and animals without being noticed.

- Try not to let your shadow fall on rock pools, as it will give you away and creatures will hide from you!

BEACHCOMBING

Beach finds include smooth driftwood, shells, pebbles, crab claws, feathers, and seaweed. Collect your finds in a bucket. Can you identify them all? Remember to return them to the beach when you're finished.

GLOSSARY

Anchor to hold something firmly in place.

Antennae the "feelers" on an insect's head, which are used for sensing.

Burrow a hole or tunnel in the ground where a small animal might live.

Carnivore an animal that eats mainly meat.

Crustacean one of a group of animals with many legs and a hard body case, such as lobsters, crabs, and shrimps.

Dune a mound of wind-blown sand.

Frond part of a seaweed that is like a stem with leaves.

Habitat the natural home of plants or animals, such as a wood or a pond.

Herbivore an animal that eats mainly plants.

Holdfast a root-like part used by seaweed to anchor onto rocks.

Minibeast a small animal that doesn't have a backbone, such as a butterfly or spider.

Mollusk a shelled animal, such as a clam or cockle.

Plankton tiny floating plants and animals.

Predator an animal that hunts another animal for food.

Prey an animal that is hunted by another animal for food.

Scavenge to feed off waste and scraps

Tentacle a long feeler, used by an animal for sensing or to capture its food.

Tide the rise and fall in sea level on the coast.

Webbed feet when an animal has skin between its toes, so its feet work like paddles.

FIND OUT MORE

Books

The Great Outdoors: The Seashore by Lisa Regan (Franklin Watts, 2020)

Above, Below and Long Ago by Michael Bright (Wayland, 2024)

My Nature Collection: Under the Sea by Cameron Menzies (Wayland, 2025)

Websites

www.nationaltrust.org.uk/discover/nature/coast
Visit the National Trust's coast web page to find out more about rock pools, seashore sounds, and how to spot fossils at the coast.

www.audubon.org/bird-guide
The National Audubon Society's website is a great resource for identifying seashore birds.

NOTE: Every effort has been made by the Publishers to ensure that the websites on page 31 of this book are suitable for children, that they are of the highest educational value, and that they contain no inappropriate or offensive material. However, because of the nature of the Internet, it is impossible to guarantee that the contents of these sites will not be altered. We strongly advise that Internet access is supervised by a responsible adult.

INDEX